SPEAK BUSINESS GERMAN

PERFECT YOUR SPOKEN GERMAN FOR WORK

OPPIAN

Published by Oppian Press
Helsinki, 2020

ISBN 978-951-877-168-8

How to use this book

Speaking a foreign language can be daunting, even for somebody who understands spoken language pretty well. Yet being able to converse with others in their native tongue is a vital skill, not least in a business environment.

This book contains 25 useful and unique exercises for advanced learners of German. All exercises are dialogues that take place in a business setting. So grab a friend or a fellow student and start improving your German today!

The way to use the book is simple: each dialogue has two speakers, A and B. Let's say you are A and your partner is B and you want to try dialogue number 4.

First make a copy of the dialogue. You will keep the page Dialogue 4 • A to yourself and give the page Dialogue 4 • B to your partner.

On top of the page you can see a short description of the setting and the speakers. Below that you will see your lines in English. Go ahead and try to say the lines in German. Please remember, that the important thing is to convey the meaning, not to get hung up on individual words.

Your partner will see a German version of your lines on his page, so they can help you with hints if you get stuck or some words are unfamiliar to you.

Likewise, you will see German versions of their lines on your page, so you can help him as well.

After you have completed the exercise, just swap pages and roles. Now it's your turn to be B!

We hope this book will be useful to you and help you be successful in your chosen career.

DIALOGUE 1 • A

A is a receptionist at a hotel and B is the customer who wants to check in. B wants to make sure the room is quiet and needs further information on the hotel facilities.

A: Good afternoon.

B: Hallo. Ich möchte bitte gerne einchecken.

A: Certainly, what is your name?

B: B Jones.

A: Alright, I can see in the computer that you made your booking online so the room has already been paid for. I will however, need a credit card and a form of identification from you so that I can keep them on file for any additional expenses.

B: Was meinen Sie mit "zusätzliche Ausgaben"?

A: They are products and services that are not included in the room rate including room service, mini-bar items, internet and movies. We won't charge anything until you check out, however we need to register your method of payment as security.

B: Das ist in Ordnung. Hier ist mein Ausweis und meine Kreditkarte. Ich habe mich gefragt, welche Zimmertypen verfügbar sind, weil ich ganz früh am Morgen eine Konferenz habe, und ich wäre Ihnen sehr dankbar, wenn ich ein ruhiges Zimmer bekommen könnte.

A: I have a room on the second floor that is very quiet. Unfortunately it does not have a view, but it is far away from the street and the elevators.

B: Das ist okay, Aussicht ist nicht wichtig für mich. Wie kann ich mich ins WLAN einloggen?

A: If you open your browser there will be a form asking for your room number and your surname. Once you accept the terms and conditions the service will be added to your credit card charges.

B: Wann und wo wird das Frühstück serviert?

A: Buffet breakfast is served in the restaurant on the fifth floor from 7am to 9:30 am. However, the restaurant does provide a-la-carte service of breakfast after that.

B: Ok. Vielen Dank für die Informationen.

A: You are very welcome. If you have any further questions just dial 1 on the phone in your room. The elevator is just down the hall, your room is number 206 and it is located on the second floor. I hope that you will enjoy your stay with us.

DIALOGUE 1 • B

A is a receptionist at a hotel and B is the customer who wants to check in. B wants to make sure the room is quiet and needs further information on the hotel facilities.

A: Guten Tag.

B: Hello. I'd like to check in please.

A: Aber gerne doch. Wie ist Ihr Name?

B: B Jones.

A: Sehr schön. Ich sehe hier in meinem Computer, dass Sie die das Zimmer online gebucht haben und es also schon bezahlt ist. Ich brauche aber trotzdem noch Ihre Kreditkarte und einen Ausweis, damit ich diese Informationen parat habe, sollten Sie zusätzliche Ausgaben haben.

B: What do you mean by "additional expenses"?

A: Es gibt Produkte und Dienstleistungen, die nicht im Zimmerpreis inklusive sind, z.B. Zimmerservice, Artikel aus der Minibar, Internet und Filme. Wir belasten Ihre Karte nicht bis Sie auschecken, aber aus Sicherheitsgründen benötigen wir die Zahlungsinformation.

B: That's ok. Here are my passport and credit card. I was wondering which rooms are available because I have an early morning meeting and I would really appreciate it if I could have a quiet room.

A: Ich habe ein Zimmer im zweiten Stock das sehr ruhig ist. Es hat allerdings keine Aussicht, ist dafür aber sehr weit entfernt von der Straße und den Aufzügen.

B: That's fine, the view is not important to me. How can I connect to the Wi-Fi network?

A: Wenn Sie Ihren Browser aufmachen, erscheint ein Formular, das Sie nach Ihrer Zimmernummer und Ihrem Nachnamen fragt. Sobald Sie die allgemeinen Geschäftsbedingungen akzeptiert haben, werden diese Gebühren einfach zu Ihren Kreditkartenausgaben addiert.

B: When and where will breakfast be served?

A: Ein Büffet Frühstück wird im Restaurant im fünften Stock von 7.00Uhr bis 9.30Uhr morgens serviert. Das Restaurant bietet aber auch Frühstücksgerichte nach Wahl nach 9.30Uhr an.

B: Ok. Thank you for the information.

A: Gern geschehen. Wenn Sie noch irgendwelche anderen Fragen haben, wählen Sie einfach 1 auf Ihrem Zimmertelefon. Der Aufzug ist einfach den Gang entlang, Ihre Zimmernummer ist 206 und befindet sich im zweiten Stock. Ich wünsche Ihnen einen angenehmen Aufenthalt bei uns.

DIALOGUE 2 • A

A is an assistant at a construction company and B is a business journalist who wants to speak with the company's CEO about the company's latest financial results.

A: Grey Construction, how may I direct your call?

B: Hallo, mein Name ist B Marks von der Business Weekly. Wir arbeiten gerade an einem Artikel über einige der dramatischsten Geschäftsentwicklungen hier bei uns in der Stadt, und wir würden dazu gerne ein Statement von Ihrem Geschäftsführer haben.

A: Our CEO is currently in a meeting and unable to take calls. Would you like to leave a message?

B: Könnten Sie mir vielleicht seine Durchwahl geben, damit ich ihn dann einfach später direkt noch einmal anrufen kann? Oder vielleicht seine Emailadresse, damit ich ihm meine Fragen schicken kann?

A: I am sorry, but I am unable to disclose that information at this time. However, I would be more than happy to write down some further details and pass them on to him as soon as he becomes available.

B: Ok. Wir sind eine der bekanntesten Wirtschaftspublikationen hier in unserer Gegend. Ihre aktuellsten Finanzberichte haben eine beeindruckende Verbesserung aufgewiesen und wir würden Ihnen gerne ein paar Fragen stellen bezüglich Ihres Erfolgsrezeptes.

A: That sounds very interesting. I will pass your details on to our CEO and as soon as I have his answer I will contact you with further details. Could you please provide a phone number that I can reach you on and I will be sure to call you by the end of the day.

B: Ja, aber gerne. Meine Nummer ist 617 636 5477 und nochmal, mein Name ist B Marks.

A: Thank you, I will be in touch this afternoon.

B: Ich freue mich schon. Vielen Dank für Ihre Hilfe.

DIALOGUE 2 • B

A is an assistant at a construction company and B is a business journalist who wants to speak with the company's CEO about the company's latest financial results.

A: Grey Construction, wie kann ich Ihnen helfen?

B: Hello, this is B Marks from the Business Weekly. We are currently preparing an article outlining some of the city's' most dramatic business turnarounds and we'd like to request a statement from your CEO.

A: Unser Geschäftsführer ist gerade in einer Sitzung und kann keine Telefonate entgegennehmen. Möchten Sie eine Nachricht hinterlassen?

B: Is there any chance that you could give me his extension so that I can call him at a later time? Or perhaps him email address so that I can send him my questions?

A: Es tut mir leid, aber diese Informationen kann ich derzeit leider nicht freigeben. Ich kann aber gerne weitere Details aufschreiben und an ihn weitergeben, sobald er wieder verfügbar ist.

B: OK. We are one of the most prominent business publications in the area. Your latest financial reports displayed an impressive improvement and we would like to ask a few questions regarding what the recipe for success has been.

A: Das hört sich sehr interessant an. Ich werde Ihre Nachricht an unseren Geschäftsführer weitergeben und sobald ich seine Antwort habe, werde ich mich wieder bei Ihnen melden. Können Sie mir bitte Ihre Telefonnummer geben unter der ich Sie erreichen kann, und ich werde Sie spätestens heute Abend zurückrufen.

B: Yes of course. My number is 617 636 5477 and once again, my name is B Marks.

A: Vielen Dank, und ich melde mich heute Nachmittag.

B: I look forward to it. Thank you for your help.

.

DIALOGUE 3 • A

A has just missed a flight. B is the airline customer service agent at the airport.

A: Hi, I've just arrived at the airport after my taxi was caught in a traffic jam and realised that I have missed my flight to Munich. Could I please book a seat on the next available flight?

B: Das tut mir so leid. Ich werde mein bestes versuchen, Ihnen zu helfen und Ihre Reise etwas stressfreier zu machen! Kann ich bitte Ihren Ausweis sehen?

A: Of course. Here you go.

B: Vielen Dank. Ich sehe Sie haben Ihren Flug in unserem Büro in Berlin gebucht. Die guten Nachrichten sind, dass Ihr Ticket ein „Flexible Plus" Ticket ist und Sie sich deshalb für das Flug verpasst Feature qualifizieren.

A: What does that mean?

B: Das heißt, dass Sie nicht den Gesamtpreis des neuen Tickets zahlen müssen. Sie müssen nur die Differenz zahlen plus 60 Euro Umbuchungsgebühr.

A: That is good news.

B: Leider habe ich auch schlechte Nachrichten. Es gibt keine weiteren Flüge nach München bis morgen früh um 8:10Uhr.

A: I guess that I will have to book a seat on that flight then. How much will that cost?

B: Es gibt einen Gangplatz auf dem 8:10Uhr Flug direkt nach München morgen früh. Der Preis ist 524 Euro, was 104 Euro mehr ist als Ihr ursprüngliches Ticket. Das heißt, inklusive der Umbuchungsgebühr sind Sie dann bei 164 Euro.

A: OK. Please book the seat for me. Here is my credit card. Also, could you please tell me if there is a good hotel nearby?

B: Es gibt zwei Hotels direkt auf dem Flughafengelände. Eines ist ein 4 Sterne Hilton Hotel und das andere ist etwas günstiger. Wir empfehlen unseren Passagieren immer das Hilton, weil es Teil unseres Alliance Programmes ist. Dort gibt es außerdem einen kostenlosen Flughafen Shuttle Service zu den Abflugterminals und Sie erhalten Vielfliegerpunkte bei der Buchung.

A: Are you able to make the booking for me from here and how can I get there?

B: Leider kann ich die Buchung nicht hier machen. Aber wenn Sie hier zum Ausgang gehen, ganz am Ende des Ganges ist ein Informationsschalter. Dort können Sie eine Reservierung machen, und die Taxihaltestelle ist auch direkt hinter demselben Ausgang.

A: OK. Thank you very much for all your help.

DIALOGUE 3 • B

A has just missed a flight. B is the airline customer service agent at the airport.

A: Hi, ich bin gerade erst am Flughafen angekommen nachdem mein Taxi im Stau steckengeblieben ist, und jetzt habe ich meinen Flug nach München verpasst. Könnte ich bitte einen Platz auf dem nächsten verfügbaren Flug buchen?

B: I am very sorry to hear that. I will do my best to assist you and make this journey less stressful! May I have your passport please?

A: Natürlich, gerne! Hier bitte.

B: Thank you. I see here that you made your booking at our Berlin office and the good news is that your "flexible plus" ticket fare qualifies for the missed flight feature.

A: Und was heißt das?

B: This means that you do not have to pay for the full price of the new ticket. Instead, you will be charged for any difference in the fare price plus a 60 euro rescheduling penalty.

A: Na das hört sich ja gut an.

B: Unfortunately, I also have bad news. There are no more flights to Munich scheduled until tomorrow morning at 08:10.

A: Dann muss ich wohl einen Platz auf dem Flug buchen. Wieviel kostet das dann?

B: There is an aisle seat available on the 08:10 flight direct to Munich tomorrow morning. The fare price is 524 euros which is 104 euros more than your initial fare. This will bring your total to 164 euros including the penalty.

A: Gut. Bitte buchen Sie diesen Platz für mich. Hier ist meine Kreditkarte. Können Sie mir bitte auch sagen, welches Hotel hier in der Nähe gut ist?

B: There are two hotels located on airport premises. One is a 4-star Hilton and the other is a more budget friendly option. We recommend the Hilton to our passengers because they are part of our alliance program. They offer a free shuttle service to the departures terminal and you receive frequent flyer points when booking.

A: Können Sie die Buchung hier für mich machen? Und wie komme ich zum Hotel?

B: Unfortunately, I am unable to make the booking. However, on your way to the exit at the end of the hall you will see an information desk. Somebody at the desk will be able to make the reservation for you and there is a taxi bay immediately behind the same exit doors.

A: Ok. Vielen Dank nochmal für Ihre Hilfe.

DIALOGUE 4 • A

A is on a business trip and wants to rent a car for three days. B is an employee of the car rental company.

A: Hello, I'd like to rent a car and was wondering if you could assist me.

B: Aber gerne doch. Darf ich bitte Ihren Führerschein sehen? Und brauchen Sie das Auto gleich heute?

A: Yes, I need it immediately and I need it for three days.

B: Planen Sie, das Auto hier bei dieser Vermietstelle zurückzugeben oder bei einer unserer anderen landesweiten Abgabestellen?

A: I will return the car here.

B: Hätten Sie lieber ein Fahrzeug mit manuellem oder automatischem Getriebe?

A: Automatic. Also, I would like something that is suitable for business travel. I don't need a large vehicle but I do prefer a 4-door car.

B: Wenn wir all Ihre Wünsche und Präferenzen berücksichtigen, dann denke ich gibt es ein paar gute Optionen, die wir derzeit verfügbar habe. Der Chrysler oder Toyota für 49 Dollar am Tag oder der Nissan für 59 Dollar am Tag. Wir haben diese Autos alle hier bereit für Sie, wenn Sie sie gerne vorher ansehen wollen.

A: There is no need, I would like to rent the Chrysler please. Does the car come fully insured?

B: Wir bieten einen vollständigen Versicherungsschutz für nur 30 Dollar extra an. Das deckt dann Kollision, Unfallschaden, etc. bis zu einem Wert von 100 Tausend Dollar. In dieser Broschüre können Sie noch nähere Informationen dazu finden.

A: Please sign me up for the complete cover.

B: Aber gerne doch. Ihr Gesamtbetrag ist dann bei 177 Dollar. Könnte ich bitte Ihre Kreditkarte haben, wir belasten diesen Betrag, werden ihn jedoch erst abbuchen, wenn Sie das Auto am Donnerstag zurückbringen, jederzeit zwischen 7.00Uhr morgens und 18:00Uhr Abends. Bitte vergessen Sie auch nicht, dass Sie das Auto vollgetankt zurückbringen müssen. Hier sind Ihre Unterlagen, bitte unterschreiben Sie hier auf dieser Kopie, die andere sollten Sie im Auto behalten.

A: Thank you for your help.

B: Kein Problem. Ich werde jemanden schicken um das Auto zu Ihnen zu bringen, dauert nur ein paar Minuten. Einen schönen Tag noch, und fahren Sie vorsichtig!

DIALOGUE 4 • B

A is on a business trip and wants to rent a car for three days. B is an employee of the car rental company.

A: Guten Tag. Ich würde gerne ein Auto mieten. Können Sie mir dabei helfen?

B: It would be my pleasure. May I please see your drivers' license? And will you be renting the vehicle starting today?

A: Ja, ich brauche es ab sofort und für drei Tage.

B: Do you intend to return the vehicle to this centre or to another one of our nationwide drop-off centres?

A: Ich werde das Auto hier zurückgeben.

B: Do you prefer a manual or automatic transmission?

A: Automatisch. Ich hätte außerdem gerne ein Auto, das gut für Geschäftsreisen ist. Ich brauche kein großes Fahrzeug, aber ich hätte schon gerne einen 4-Türer.

B: I've taken your needs and preferences into consideration and I can recommend a couple of options that are currently available. The Chrysler or Toyota at 49 dollars a day or the Nissan for 59 dollars a day. They are all in our caryard if you would like to take a look.

A: Nein Danke, das ist nicht nötig. Ich hätte gerne den Chrysler. Kommt das Auto komplett mit Versicherung?

B: We offer complete insurance coverage at an extra 30 dollars and that will cover all collisions, accidental damage etc. to a value of 100 thousand dollars. You can see more details in this pamphlet.

A: Dann hätte ich bitte auch gerne die Komplettversicherung dazu.

B: Certainly. Your total comes to 177 dollars. If I may please have your credit card I will place a hold to this amount which will not be deducted until you return the vehicle, which can be any time on Thursday between 7 am and 6 pm. Also, please note that you are required to return the car with the fuel tank refilled. Here is your paperwork, please sign this copy and retain the other copy to keep in the car at all times.

A: Vielen Dank für Ihre Hilfe.

B: You are very welcome. I will send somebody to bring your car around to the entrance in a minute. Have a lovely day and drive safely!

DIALOGUE 5 • A

A is a customs and immigration agent at an international border. B is a business visitor.

A: May I see your passport?

B: Aber gerne doch.

A: Do you have a valid visa to enter our country?

B :   Ja, ich habe ein Visa, Sie können es in meinem Ausweis sehen.

A: What is the purpose of your visit?

B: Ich arbeite für ein internationales Modelabel und ich bin hier, um einigen Einzelhandelsgeschäften unsere neue Kollektion anzubieten.

A: How long will you be staying here and where will you be residing?

B: 10 Tage und ich werde im Superb Hotel in Bigtown übernachten.

A: Could I see your return ticket and your reservation details if you have them printed please?

B: Ich habe meine Hotelbuchung nicht ausgedruckt, aber ich habe die Bestätigung in einer Email auf meinem Handy, aber ich habe gerade keinen Internetzugang.

A: That's ok, the return ticket is fine. How do you intend to finance your time here?

B: Ich habe eine Firmenkreditkarte und ausreichend Bargeld für persönliche Ausgaben.

A: Are you carrying any goods that you plan to distribute or sell while here?

B: Nein, nur Warenmuster.

A: OK, everything seems to be in order. Welcome and enjoy your stay.

DIALOGUE 5 • B

A is a customs and immigration agent at an international border. B is a business visitor.

A: Darf ich bitte Ihren Ausweis sehen?

B: Yes, of course.

A: Haben Sie ein gültiges Visa zur Einreise in unser Land?

B :   Yes, I have a visa, you will see it in my passport.

A: Was ist der Zweck Ihres Besuches?

B: I work for an international fashion label and I am here to offer our new collection to several retail stores.

A: Wie lange haben Sie vor hier zu bleiben und wo werden Sie wohnen?

B: 10 days and I will be staying at the Superb Hotel in Bigtown.

A: Darf ich bitte Ihr Rückflugticket und Ihre Reservierungsinformation sehen, falls Sie sie ausgedruckt haben?

B: I do not have my hotel booking printed, I have the confirmation in an email on my mobile phone but I do not currently have internet access.

A: Das ist in Ordnung, das Rückflugticket reicht aus. Wie haben Sie vor Ihren Aufenthalt hier zu finanzieren?

B: I have a company credit card and sufficient cash for personal costs.

A: Bringen Sie irgendwelche Waren mit sich, die Sie verteilen oder verkaufen wollen, während Sie hier sind?

B: No, only sample products.

A: Gut, alles scheint in Ordnung zu sein. Willkommen und einen schönen Aufenthalt.

DIALOGUE 6 • A

A is a business traveller whose luggage has disappeared. B is a customer service agent at the airport.

A: Hi, could you please help me? My luggage hasn't arrived on the carousel.

B: Das tut mir aber leid. Kann ich bitte Ihren Ausweis sehen? Und auf welchem Flieger sind Sie angekommen?

A: The EK420 from Dubai.

B: Sind Sie direkt aus Dubai angekommen oder sind Sie noch an einem anderen Ort umgestiegen?

A: I began my journey in Zurich.

B: Es ist möglich, dass Ihr Gepäck die erste Verbindung nicht geschafft hat, es wird jedoch noch hier ankommen. Um Ihren Antrag zu bearbeiten, muss ich Ihnen einige Fragen stellen, damit wir Ihr Gepäck besser identifizieren können. Wieviele Gepäckstücke fehlen?

A: Two. I have name tags on both of them.

B: Können Sie bitte die Gepäckstücke für mich beschreiben, Größe, Farbe, Material und Muster oder Hersteller?

A: They are both Samsonite, plain black bags. The name tags are bright red tags. I'm not sure about the dimensions, they are large suitcases.

B: Vielen Dank. Bitte füllen Sie dieses Formular aus und geben Sie die Adresse an, an die Sie die Koffer geliefert haben möchten, sobald Sie ankommen. Dann unterschreiben Sie bitte ganz unten, nachdem Sie die allgemeinen Geschäftsbedingungen gelesen haben. Bitte geben Sie auch eine örtliche Telefonnummer an, unter der wir Sie erreichen können, falls es Probleme gibt.

A: When can I expect my bags to arrive?

B: Wir werden unser bestes versuchen, sie innerhalb der nächsten 72 Stunden zu liefern.

A: OK, thank you.

DIALOGUE 6 • B

A is a business traveller whose luggage has disappeared. B is a customer service agent at the airport.

A: Hi, können Sie mir bitte helfen? Mein Gepäck ist nicht beim Gepäckförderband angekommen.

B: I am sorry to hear that. Can I see your passport, please? And which flight did you arrive on?

A: Auf EK420 aus Dubai.

B: Did you arrive directly from Dubai or did your flight connect from another destination?

A: Ich bin in Zürich losgeflogen.

B: There is a possibility that your luggage did not make the initial connection, however it will eventually arrive here. In order to process this claim I will need to ask you a few questions to help us identify your bags. How many pieces of luggage are missing?

A: Zwei. Und ich habe an beiden Namensschilder.

B: Could you please describe the bags including their size, colour, material and any patterns or brand names?

A: Es sind beide Samsonite, ganz schwarz. Die Namensschilder sind leuchtend rot. Ich bin mir nicht sicher über die Größe, sie sind ziemlich groß.

B: Thank you. Please fill out this form stating the address to which you would like us to deliver your luggage once it arrives and sign the bottom once you have read the terms and conditions. Make sure that you also provide a local phone number so that we can reach you if any issues arise.

A: Wann kommen meine Koffer ungefähr an?

B: We will do our best to deliver them within the next 72 hours.

A: OK, vielen Dank.

DIALOGUE 7 • A

A is an art director for a graphic design firm, and B is her client. B asks A to make some tweaks in the new marketing material, and wants to know if she can get the work done by tomorrow.

A: Hi B. Thanks for the draft marketing materials you sent through yesterday afternoon. We love the design and layout of everything, and the new logo is exactly what we were looking for. We're not so sure about the colour scheme in the corporate brochure though, and some of the images aren't quite right for our brand either.

B: Na gut. Das hört sich so an, als ob wir einige Dinge etwas anpassen müssen. Welche Bilder genau waren es, bei denen Sie sich nicht ganz sicher sind?

A: The ones on pages 3, 9 and 11. The rest are fine, but we'd rather use something a bit more targeted on these pages, to better illustrate the messages in the copy. Perhaps some shots of our products, or members of our sales team meeting with clients. I can give you access to our online image library; I'm sure you'll be able to find some suitable shots in there.

B: Okay, natürlich. Bitte emailen Sie mir den Link und ich sehe sie mir gleich mal an. Was haben Sie sich bezüglich der Farbenwahl gedacht? Hätten Sie lieber etwas dezenteres, oder einfach komplett andere Farben?

A: We do like the colours, but the shades are a bit too bold for us. We're targeting a business audience and we want a more professional look. Could you have them toned down a bit please? I'll send you our branding style guide so you can see which pantones we usually use.

B: Das ware sehr hilfreich, vielen Dank.

A: OK great. That's all really, just those tweaks to make. We've got to get drafts of these documents in front of the directors on Wednesday morning for approval. Is there any chance you can prioritise these changes please, and send me through an updated version of the brochure by tomorrow?

B: Ja, das ist definitiv möglich, wenn Sie mir den Style Guide und den Link für die Bildergalerie noch heute Morgen schicken können.

A: Great, thanks. I'll email them to you right away. Call me if you need any clarification. I look forward to seeing the final draft tomorrow.

B: Vielen Dank A. Auf Wiederhören.

DIALOGUE 7 • B

A is an art director for a graphic design firm, and B is her client. B asks A to make some tweaks in the new marketing material, and wants to know if she can get the work done by tomorrow.

A: Hi B. Vielen Dank für den Entwurf des Marketing Materials, das Sie mir gestern geschickt haben. Das Design und Layout sind wirklich toll, und das neue Logo ist genau das, was wir wollten. Wir sind uns aber nicht ganz sicher über die Farbwahl in der Firmenbroschüre, und ein paar von den Bildern sind nicht genau das richtige für unsere Marke.

B: OK, it sounds like we need to make some adjustments then. Which images are you uncertain about?

A: Die auf den Seiten 3, 9 und 11. Die anderen sind in Ordnung. Aber auf diesen Seiten würden wir lieber etwas benützen, das zielorientierter ist, damit die Nachricht in der Broschüre besser vermittelt wird. Vielleicht ein paar Aufnahmen von unseren Produkten, oder Mitglieder von unserem Verkaufsteam während einem Kundengespräch. Ich kann Ihnen Zugang zu unserer online Bildergalerie geben, ich bin mir sicher, dass Sie dort etwas passendes finden können.

B: OK, of course. Please email me the link and I'll look through them right away. So what are your thoughts on the colour scheme? Would you prefer something more subtle, or do you want different colours altogether?

A: Die Farben an sich gefallen uns schon, aber die Nuancen sind ein bißchen zu gewagt für uns. Unsere Zielgruppe sind Geschäftsleute und wir hätten deshalb gerne einen etwas seriöseren Look. Könnten Sie die Farben bitte ein wenig dämpfen? Ich schicke Ihnen auch unseren Branding Style Guide, damit Sie sehen, welche Pantone wir normalerweise benützen.

B: That would be really helpful. Thank you.

A: Okay, großartig. Das ist eigentlich alles, nur diese zwei kleinen Änderungen. Wir müssen die Auswürfe dieser Dokumente am Mittwoch morgen den Abteilungsleitern vorlegen zur Genehmigung. Ist es irgendwie möglich, dass Sie diesen Änderungen den Vorrang geben können, bitte, und mir die überarbeitete Version der Broschüre spätestens morgen schicken können?

B: Yes, I can definitely do that, provided that you can get that style guide and the link for the image library over to me this morning.

A: Super, vielen Dank. Ich schicke die Email gleich los. Rufen Sie mich an, falls Sie irgendwelche Fragen haben. Ich freue mich schon, den Entwurf morgen zu sehen.

B: Thanks A. Bye for now.

DIALOGUE 8 • A

A is on his way to a business meeting with B, but his car has broken down. A calls B to apologise and asks if B wants to reschedule the meeting.

A: Hi B, this is A. I'm so sorry, but I'm running late for our meeting this morning. My car has broken down on the highway, and I'm waiting for roadside assistance.

B: Das ist ärgerlich. Können Sie mir ungefähr sagen, wie lange es dauern wird?

A: Apparently the response time is up to an hour, so even if they can get it running right away I doubt I could be there until 1 pm at the earliest. Would it suit you to meet this afternoon instead, or would you prefer to reschedule.

B: Einen Moment, ich muss kurz meinen Terminplaner checken. Ich sehe ihn mir schnell auf dem Bildschirm hier an.

A: OK, thanks

B: Okay, also es sieht so aus, als ob wir heute nachmittag einen neuen Kunden treffen, das heißt, heute nachmittag geht für uns nicht. Wir müssen es wohl auf einen anderen Tag verschieben. Aber wir haben ein paar ziemlich dringende Dinge zu besprechen, deswegen wäre so bald wie möglich am besten.

A: Yes, we need to go over those year-end procedures as soon as possible, and review progress on the marketing project. The deadline is only two weeks away so we've no time to waste. Are you free tomorrow morning?

B: Da sieht es auch ziemlich voll aus, aber ich könnte Sie eventuell zwischenrein schieben, wenn Sie ganz früh hier sein können. Wie wäre es mit einem Frühstückstreffen, um 8 Uhr? Ich bin mir nicht sicher, ob meine Kollegen so früh können, aber ich kann sie ja immer noch später briefen.

A: Yes, I can make 8 am tomorrow. Do you want to meet at your offices?

B: Ja, aber der Empfang ist so früh noch nicht besetzt. Können Sie mich bitte auf meinem Handy anrufen, wenn Sie ankommen, dann komme ich hinunter und lasse Sie hinein. Haben Sie die Nummer?

A: Yes, I do. Thanks so much for your flexibility. I'll see you in the morning.

B: Vielen Dank auch. Bis morgen.

DIALOGUE 8 • B

A is on his way to a business meeting with B, but his car has broken down. A calls B to apologise and asks if B wants to reschedule the meeting.

A: Hi B, A am Apparat. Es tut mir so leid, aber ich bin etwas spät für unser Treffen heute morgen. Mein Auto hat auf der Autobahn den Geist aufgegeben und ich warte auf den Pannendienst.

B: That's frustrating. Have you any idea how long you'll be?

A: Anscheinend ist die Antwortzeit bis zu einer Stunde, das heißt, selbst wenn sie es sofort richten können, bezweifle ich, dass ich vor 13Uhr frühestens da sein kann. Würde es heute nachmittag für Sie auch gehen, oder möchten Sie lieber komplett verschieben?

B: Hang on. Let me check my diary. I'll just pull it up on my screen.

A: Okay, vielen Dank.

B: It looks like we've got a new client coming in after lunch, so I'm afraid I won't be able to see you this afternoon. We'll have to move it to another day. But we've got some quite urgent matters to cover, so let's make it as soon as possible.

A: Ja, wir müssen noch über die Jahresabschlussvorgänge gehen, und zwar so bald wie möglich, und den Fortschritt bei den Marketing Projekten besprechen. Die Deadline ist in zwei Wochen, wir haben also keine Zeit zu verschwenden. Haben Sie morgen früh Zeit?

B: It's looking quite busy, but I could squeeze you in if you can make it early. How about a breakfast meeting at 8 am? I'm not sure if any of my colleagues will be able to join us at that hour, but I can always brief them afterwards.

A: Ja, morgen um 8Uhr past. Wollen Sie sich in Ihrem Büro treffen?

B: Yes, although reception won't be manned at that hour. Can you please call me on my mobile when you get here, and I'll come down and let you in. You have the number?

A: Ja, ich habe sie. Vielen Dank für Ihre Flexibilität. Bis morgen früh dann.

B: Thanks. See you then.

DIALOGUE 9 • A

A calls the company helpline because she cannot log into her online account. B is the customer care specialist helping her. They figure out that A has caps lock on her keyboard and that's why her password is not accepted.

A: IT helpline. This is A speaking. How can I help you today?

B: Hi A. Mein Name ist B und ich arbeite in der Buchhaltung. Ich versuche jetzt seit zehn Minuten mich in meinem Konto in unserem Firmenintranet anzumelden, aber mein Passwort wird immer wieder abgelehnt. Ich bin mir sicher, dass es das richtige ist, und gestern hat es noch perfekt funktioniert. Ich weiß einfach nicht, was das Problem ist. Jetzt habe ich eine Nachricht bekommen, dass ich gesperrt wurde. Können Sie mir helfen?

A: OK B, let's take a look. Can you give me your surname please so I can find you on the system?

B: Mein Name ist Smith.

A: Ah yes. I've found you. And can you tell me what username you've typed in?

B: Einen Moment, ich schaue schnell. Ich habe eine Automatische Füll Funktion für dieses Feld, damit ich es nicht jedesmal eintippen muss... Okay, es ist asmith, dann das „at" Zeichen, dann company Punkt com. Ich ändere es aber nie, es muss also richtig sein.

A: OK, yes, that's the right format, so that's not the problem. I can see that you've made several log-on attempts in the last quarter of an hour. You've exceeded the maximum number – for security reasons you get locked out after 5.

B: Und was mache ich jetzt?

A: Don't worry, I can reset it from here. I'll give you a temporary password so you can log on, but you'll need to change that immediately, ok?

B: Aber sicher doch. Was ist das neue Passwort?

A: I've reset it to 'smith', all lower case. Can you try it?

B: Ich tippe es gerade ein. Nein! Hat mich schon wieder abgelehnt!

A: It's case sensitive. Perhaps your Caps Lock is on. Could you please check?

B: Oh! Ja, das ist es! Das war wahrscheinlich die ganze Zeit das Problem. Ich versuche das neue Passwort nochmal...Ja, ich bin drin! Vielen Dank.

A: That's a pleasure. Glad I could help. Don't forget to choose a new password immediately. Is there anything else I can help you with today?

B: Nein Danke, A. Vielen Dank für Ihre Hilfe. Auf Wiederhören.

DIALOGUE 9 • B

A calls the company helpline because she cannot log into her online account. B is the customer care specialist helping her. They figure out that A has caps lock on her keyboard and that's why her password is not accepted.

A: IT Beratungsstelle. Mein Name ist A. Wie kann ich Ihnen heute behilflich sein?

B: Hi A. My name's B and I work in the Accounts department. I've been trying for ten minutes to log onto my account on the company intranet, but it keeps rejecting my password. I'm sure it's the right one, and it worked fine yesterday so I can't figure out what's going on. Now I've got a message saying I've been locked out. Can you help?

A: OK B, schauen wir uns das mal an. Können Sie mir bitte Ihren Nachnamen geben, damit ich Sie im System finden kann?

B: It's Smith.

A: Ah ja. Ich habe Sie gefunden. Und können Sie mir bitte sagen, welchen Benutzernamen Sie eingegeben haben?

B: Hang on let me check. There's an autofill on that field so I don't have to type it in every time… OK, It's bsmith, then an 'at' sign, then company dot com. I never change it though, so I'm sure its right.

A: Okay, ja, das ist das richtige Format, also ist dies nicht das Problem. Ich kann hier sehen, dass Sie ein paar Einloggversuche gemacht haben, alle in der letzten viertel Stunde. Sie haben die Maximalanzahl überschritten. Aus Sicherheitsgründen werden Sie nach 5 Versuchen gesperrt.

B: So what can I do?

A: Keine Sorge, ich kann es von hier aus zurücksetzen. Ich gebe Ihnen ein temporäres Passwort damit Sie sich anmelden können, aber Sie müssen es dann sofort ändern, okay?

B: Sure. What's the new password?

A: Ich habe es auf ´smith´ zurückgesetzt, alles in Kleinbuchstaben. Können Sie das mal ausprobieren?

B: Typing it in now. No! It rejected me again!

A: Es ist wichtig, auf Groß- und Kleinschreibung zu achten. Vielleicht ist Ihre Feststelltaste gedrückt. Können Sie das bitte mal überprüfen?

B: Oh! It is! That must have been the problem all along. I'll try the new password again… Yes, I'm in! Thank you.

A: Gern geschehen. Freut mich, dass ich Ihnen helfen konnte. Vergessen Sie nicht, sofort ein neues Passwort auszuwählen. Kann ich Ihnen heute sonst noch irgendwie weiterhelfen?

B: No, thanks A. I really appreciate your help. Bye.

DIALOGUE 10 • A

A calls B to find out if B is happy with the widgets his business purchased from A's company some time ago. B has no complaints about the product, but notes that the shipping company that A used were not quite as punctual as they should have been. A promises to use another shipping company next time.

A: Hi B. This is A from Super Widgets. This is just a courtesy call to make sure you're happy with the consignment of extra wide widgets you bought from us last month. Were you able to install them ok?

B: Hey A. Vielen Dank für Ihren Anruf. Die Widgets sind super, vielen Dank. Die Installation war problemlos, und jeder findet sie sehr benutzerfreundlich. In den ersten paar Tagen haben wir ein paar Mal beim Kundenservice angerufen, aber die waren eigentlich immer sehr hilfreich, und die Handbücher, die Sie mitgeliefert haben, sind auch sehr ausführlich.

A: Oh that's great to hear. So they are performing as you'd hoped?

B: Absolut. Das Produkt ist großartig und das Ergebnis ist genau das, was wir uns erhofft haben. Die gesamte Abteilung arbeitet viel effizienter und unsere Produktivität ist diesen Monat auch gestiegen.

A: That's excellent feedback. Thank you! I'm so glad you're happy with them. So overall, were you happy with your customer experience at Super Widgets?

B: Ja, im großen und ganzen schon. Aber, wo Sie fragen, eine Sache hat mich ein wenig enttäuscht.

A: I'm sorry to hear that! What was it?

B: Naja, wie Sie wissen, hatten wir etwas eilig mit dem Upgraden unseres Systems, und wir hatten erwartet, dass wir die Widgets innerhalb einer Woche erhalten würden. Wir waren sehr beeindruckt damit, wie schnell Sie unsere Bestellung bearbeitet haben – aber es hat mehr als 10 Tage gedauert von dem Tag, an dem Sie uns die Versandbestätigung geschickt haben,bis die Lieferung bei uns angekommen ist. Es hat unser Launchdatum verzögert und der Lieferant konnte uns keine Erklärung für die Verzögerung geben.

A: Oh I'm so sorry! That's not at all consistent with our service standards and I'm very disappointed to hear it. I'll start an investigation immediately to find out what happened, and we'll definitely use another shipping company from now on.

B: Großartig, vielen Dank. Das ist sehr nett von Ihnen, auch der Telefonanruf. Wir werden uns im nächsten Quartal wieder melden, wenn wir mit der nächsten Phase unseres Systemupgrades beginnen.

A: Thanks. I'll look forward to meeting with you then to find out how we can help.

DIALOGUE 10 • B

A calls B to find out if B is happy with the widgets his business purchased from A's company some time ago. B has no complaints about the product, but notes that the shipping company that A used were not quite as punctual as they should have been. A promises to use another shipping company next time.

A: Hi B. A am Apparat, von Super Widgets. Ich wollte nur anrufen um nachzufragen, ob Sie mit der Lieferung der extra breiten Widgets, die Sie letzten Monat von uns gekauft haben, zufrieden sind. Konnten Sie sie ohne Probleme installieren?

B: Hey A. Thanks for your call. The widgets are great, thanks. The installation was seamless, thanks, and everyone has found them very easy to use. We made a few calls to your support team in the first few days but they were really helpful, and the instruction manuals you provided with them are very thorough.

A: Oh das freut mich zu hören. Sie funktionieren also wie gewünscht?

B: Absolutely. The product is great and the outcome has been just what we were hoping for. The entire department is operating more efficiently and our productivity has been right up this month.

A: Das ist super Feedback. Vielen Dank! Ich bin so froh, dass Sie zufrieden mit Ihrem Einkauf sind. Das heißt also, dass Sie im großen und ganzen zufrieden waren mit der Kundenerfahrung bei Super Widgets?

B: Yes, on the whole. Since you're asking there was one disappointing thing though.

A: Oh, das tut mir aber leid! Was war das?

B: Well as you know, we were in a bit of a hurry to upgrade our systems and we had expected to receive the widgets within a week. We were very impressed with how fast you processed our order – but it took more than 10 days from when you sent us the shipping notice before the consignment got delivered. It held up our launch date and the courier couldn't give any explanation for the delay at all.

A: Oh das tut mir so leid. Das ist überhaupt nicht vereinbar mit unseren Servicestandards und ich bin sehr enttäuscht, das zu hören. Ich werde das sofort untersuchen und herausfinden, was passiert ist, und wir werden von nun an auf alle Fälle eine andere Versandfirma verwenden.

B: Great, thanks. I appreciate that, and the follow up call. We'll be in touch next quarter when we start on the next phase of system upgrades.

A: Vielen Dank. Ich freue mich schon, mich dann mit Ihnen zu treffen und herauszufinden, wie wir Ihnen weiterhelfen können.

DIALOGUE 11 • A

A is a software developer and B is his manager. There is a critical software bug in the latest build that A has submitted and it has crashed B's computer. A promises to come over and sort things out asap.

A: Hi B, it's A. I've just tried to run the latest version of that finance program you're working on, and it's crashed my computer. It looks like there was a critical bug of some sort in the build you submitted this morning.

B: Oh nein! Das tut mir so leid. Ich habe es eigentlich sehr gründlich getestet hier an meiner Station, bevor ich es eingereicht habe, und es ist super gelaufen. Was genau ist passiert?

A: The installation was quick and straightforward, but it crashed about 2 minutes after I started to run it. I was able to log in ok and access the main menu and setting pages, but as soon as I tried to load the bookkeeping module it just froze. My entire system is completely locked up now; it won't even shut down or restart.

B: Oh Gott. Es muss wohl irgendwie negativ mit irgendeiner anderen Software auf Deinem PC zusammenwirken. Du hast doch einige spezielle HR Management und Strategie Anwendungen, oder? Ich werde ein paar Diagnosetest machen um nach Integrationsproblemen zu suchen.

A: Ok, can you come and do that right away please? I have a budget report to prepare for the management team meeting this afternoon, so I need my system back online urgently. There's some sensitive data I need to retrieve for the report, and I have some unsaved work I really don't want to lose.

B: Okay, ich komme sofort rüber und arbeite and diesen Tests. In der Zwischenzeit klone ich Dein Profil und mache einen anderen PC für dich fertig, so dass Du arbeiten kannst, bis ich die Tests fertig durchgeführt habe und Dein System wieder neu gebooted habe. Sobald ich herausgefunden habe, was das Problem ist, werde ich anfangen, an einem Patch zu arbeiten.

A: Ok, thanks.

DIALOGUE 11 • B

A is a software developer and B is his manager. There is a critical software bug in the latest build that A has submitted and it has crashed B's computer. A promises to come over and sort things out asap.

A: Hi B, ich bin es, A. Ich habe gerade versucht, die letzte Version des Finanzprogrammes, an dem Du arbeitest, laufen zu lassen, und es hat meinen Computer gecrashed. Es sieht so aus, als ob irgendein kritischer Bug in der Version ist, die Du diesen Morgen eingereicht hast.

B: Oh no! I'm so sorry. I tested it pretty thoroughly at my station before I submitted it, and it ran like clockwork. What happened exactly?

A: Die Installation war super schnell und problemlos, aber ungefähr 2 Minuten, nachdem ich angefangen habe es laufen zu lassen, ist der Computer abgestürzt. Ich konnte mich ganz normal einloggen und hatte Zugang zum Hauptmenü und den Einstellungsseiten, aber sobald ich versucht habe, das Buchhaltungsmodul zu starten, ist der Bildschirm gefroren. Mein ganzes System ist jetzt komplett gesperrt, ich kann nicht einmal mehr ausschalten oder neustarten.

B: Oh dear. It must be interacting adversely with some of the other software on your pc. You have some specialist HR management and strategy applications don't you? I'll need to run some diagnostic tests to look for integration issues.

A: Okay, kannst Du bitte sofort kommen und das erledigen? Ich muss einen Budgetbericht für die Managementkonferenz heute nachmittag vorbereiten, deswegen muss mein System dringend wieder online sein. Es sind ein paar vertrauliche Daten, die ich für diesen Bericht benötige, und ich habe auch ungespeicherte Arbeit, die ich wirklich nicht verlieren will.

B: Right, I'll come over there straight away and run those tests. In the meantime I'll clone your profile and set you up on another PC so you can work until I can run these tests and get your system rebooted. Once I know what the problem is I'll start work on a patch.

A: Ok, Danke.

DIALOGUE 12 • A

A is a visitor who has an appointment at the marketing department. B is the receptionist who will greet him at the lobby and issue him a visitor pass.

A: Good morning sir. Welcome to Practice Corporation. How can I help you this morning?

B: Hallo. Mein Name ist B Jones. Ich habe einen Termin mit Jack Smith in der Marketing Abteilung. Ich bin leider etwas früh dran.

A: Oh yes, your name is here on our authorised visitors list. I'll just print you out a visitor's pass, so that security will let you through. Could you please fill out your details and sign the visitors' register, just in this box here? The sign in time is 10.47am.

B: Ja, kein Problem. Können Sie mir vielleicht sagen, ob irgendjemand anderes bereits für das Meeting hier ist?

A: No, you're the first to arrive, but I see from our schedule that it doesn't start until 11.30 am. I'll just call up and let Mr Smith know that you're here.

B: Großartig. Vielen Dank.

A: Oh, I'm sorry. Mr Smith's secretary informs me he's still tied up in his previous meeting but she'll inform him that you're here. I'm afraid there's another meeting taking place in the conference room at the moment, so I wonder if you'd mind taking a seat down here in the lobby for the moment.

B: Das ist überhaupt kein Problem. Ich warte einfach hier drüben. Haben Sie WLAN, damit ich arbeiten kann während ich warte?

A: Yes, certainly. Here's the network name and access password. Would you like a cup of tea or coffee while you wait?

B: Nein Danke, aber ein Glas Wasser wäre gut, bitte. Und können Sie mir bitte sagen, wo die Toiletten sind?

A: Yes it's just over there through that door behind that screen. I'll have a jug of water brought out to you right away, and just let me know if there's anything else you need.

B: Vielen Dank, dass ist sehr nett von Ihnen.

DIALOGUE 12 • B

A is a visitor who has an appointment at the marketing department. B is the receptionist who will greet him at the lobby and issue him a visitor pass.

A: Guten Morgen. Willkommen bei Practice Corporation. Wie kann ich Ihnen heute weiterhelfen?

B: Hi. My name's B Jones. I'm here for a meeting with Jack Smith in the marketing department. I'm afraid I'm running a bit early.

A: Ah ja, hier ist Ihr Name auf unserer authorisierten Besucher Liste, Herr Jones. Ich drucke Ihnen gerade schnell einen Besucherpass aus, damit unsere Sicherheitsleute Sie durchlassen. Könnten Sie bitte Ihre persönlichen Informationen ausfüllen und das Besucherregister unterschreiben, einfach nur in diesem Feld hier? Die Uhrzeit ist 10.47Uhr.

B: Yes, no problem. Could you please tell me whether anyone else has arrived for the meeting yet?

A: Nein, Sie sind der erste, aber ich sehe hier auf unserem Terminplan, dass das Meeting erst um 11:30Uhr anfängt. Ich rufe gerade mal Herr Smith an und gebe ihm Bescheid, dass Sie schon hier sind.

B: Great, thanks.

A: Oh, es tut mir leid, aber die Sekretärin von Herrn Smith hat mir gerade gesagt, dass er noch in einem anderen Meeting ist, aber sie wird ihm Bescheid geben, dass Sie hier sind. Leider ist der Konferenzraum gerade belegt, wäre es in Ordnung für Sie, wenn Sie dabei in der Lobby warten?

B: No problem, I'll just wait over there. Do you have wifi I can use, so I can work while I'm waiting?

A: Ja, natürlich. Hier ist der Name des Netzwerks und das Passwort. Möchten Sie vielleicht eine Tasse Tee oder Kaffee während Sie warten?

B: No thanks, but I'd love a drink of water please. And could you please tell me where the men's room is?

A: Ja, die Toiletten befinden sich da drüben, durch diese Tür hinter der Abtrennung. Und ich lasse gleich Wasser für Sie herausbringen, Herr Jones. Falls Sie noch irgendetwas anderes benötigen, geben Sie mir bitte Bescheid.

B: I appreciate it. Thank you.

DIALOGUE 13 • A

A and B and on their way to pitch a new product to a potential customer. They talk about their strategy and agree that B should take the lead and A should help with the technical details.

A: The taxi's here. Are you ready to go? Got everything?

B   Ja, alles fertig. Ich habe alle Produktbroschüren und die technischen Details hier bei mir, und das Informationsblatt, dass ich zusammenstellen sollte.

A: Great. What about that consumer research the marketing team were working on. Did they get it to you in time?

B: Ja, und ich habe auch die Datei mit der Berichterstattung von Jenny aus der PR Abteilung. Sieht ziemlich beeindruckend aus, wir haben einige sehr gute Rezensionen von Kunden und Kommentatoren aus dem Industriebereich bekommen.

A: Great, that will really support our pitch. These guys are quite cautious; they'll want some compelling evidence that the product lives up to our claims. So, let's talk strategy. How shall we handle this one?

B: Bisher haben sie ja nur mit Ihnen gesprochen, deswegen ist es wahrscheinlich das Beste, wenn Sie heute auch hauptsächlich das Gespräch führen. Wissen Sie, wer alles beim Meeting sein wird?

A: I've only met with Greg and Julie so far. They seem keen but the decision isn't in their hands. Their manager Phil will be there this morning, and the department head too I think. She's the one we'll have to convince.

B: OK. Sie kennen die Verkaufstaktik so gut wie kein anderer. Am besten überlasse ich Ihnen das Reden, und ich helfe dann einfach mit den Details. Ich habe mir die Details und die Verbraucherdaten gut angesehen und kann jederzeit einspringen, wenn Sie nähere Infos oder Nummern brauchen. Ich habe auch die aktuellsten Benutzerzahlen und Hochrechnungen auf meinem Laptop, falls sie danach fragen.

A: Excellent. And what about the product demo? I think you'd better run that, since you'll be able to answer any questions that come up.

B: Sicherlich. Alles ist auf meinem Laptop bereit.

A: Great. I think that's everything covered off. Let's go.

DIALOGUE 13 • B

A and B and on their way to pitch a new product to a potential customer. They talk about their strategy and agree that B should take the lead and A should help with the technical details.

A: Das Taxi ist hier. Sind Sie fertig? Alles dabei?

B   Yes, it's all ready. I've got all the product brochures and technical specifications right here, plus that fact sheet you asked me to put together.

A: Super. Was ist mit der Verbraucherforschung, an der das Marketingteam gearbeitet hat? Haben sie Ihnen das rechtzeitig gegeben?

B: Yes, and I've also got a file of media coverage from Jenny in PR. It's looking quite impressive; we're getting some very positive reviews from both customers and industry commentators.

A: Super, das wird uns bei unserem Verkaufsgespräch sehr helfen. Diese Leute sind ziemlich vorsichtig, sie werden wahrscheinlich sehr überzeugende Nachweise sehen wollen, dass unser Produkt auch wirklich bringt was es verspricht. Also, wie sieht es mit einer Strategie aus? Wie denkst Du sollten wir an das Ganze herangehen?

B: Well they've only been dealing with you up to now, so it makes sense that you take the lead. Do you know who's going to be at the meeting?

A: Ich habe bisher nur Greg und Julie getroffen. Die zwei scheinen sehr begeistert zu sein, aber die Entscheidung liegt nicht in ihren Händen. Ihr Manager Phil wird heute auch dabei sein, und der Abteilungsleiter, glaube ich. Sie ist diejenige, die wir überzeugen müssen.

B: OK. Well you know the pitch inside out. Why don't I leave most of the talking to you, and just back you up on the specifics? I've been studying these specs and the consumer data so I can jump in if you need details and numbers. I've got all the latest user figures and projections on my laptop too, in case they ask for them.

A: Super! Wie sieht es mit einer Produktdemonstration aus? Ich glaube, es ist am Besten, wenn Sie das übernehmen. Sie können mögliche Fragen am besten beantworten.

B: Sure. It's all ready to go on my laptop.

A: Großartig. Ich glaube, dann haben wir alles abgedeckt. Gehen wir!

DIALOGUE 14 • A

B is going to launch a new catering business. A is a freelance website developer. B calls to find out how much a professional website would cost her and how quickly it could be done.

A: Web Solutions, A Jackson speaking.

B: Hi A. Mein Name ist B. Ich brauche eine Website und habe Sie gerade online gefunden. Ich würde mich gerne mit Ihnen unterhalten damit Sie mir möglicherweise eine Website für mich erstellen. Wären Sie daran interessiert, mir ein Angebot zu machen?

A: Sure. What sort of thing are you looking for?

B: Also gut, ich bin gerade dabei, ein neues Catering Unternehmen zu starten und ich muss Werbung machen. Wir spezialisieren uns im Veganen Buffet Bereich und wollen deshalb am besten eine Website mit einem richtig frischen Aussehen und Flair, mit vielen Bildern von Gemüse und Früchten und anderen Zutaten.

A: OK. Have you got photos already or would you need me to source the images?

B: Wir hatten gerade einen professionellen Fotoshoot. Bilder werden also von uns bereitgestellt. Wir haben auch gerade erst kürzlich an unserem Branding gearbeitet, ich kann Ihnen also auch für das Design ein paar Ideen geben.

A: OK great. So the costs will depend on how complex the layout of the site needs to be. Have you any thoughts on what you want to include?

B: Also gut, wir brauchen auf alle Fälle eine Karte um zu zeigen, welche geographische Regionen wir bedienen. Wir benötigen auch ein paar Seiten, auf denen wir erzählen können, was wir machen, die Zutaten, die wir benützen, und vielleicht noch ein paar Beispiel Menüs. Ich hätte auch noch gerne einen Blog Bereich mit Links zu all unseren Social Media Feeds – Pinterest, Instagram, Facebook usw.

A: OK, that's all quite straightforward. Do you need the site to take bookings, or just encourage people to get in touch with their enquiries?

B: Oh nein, wir machen die Buchungen immer direkt mit dem Kunden, wir wollen also nur, dass die potentiellen Kunden uns per Telefon oder Email kontaktieren.

A: Right. That gives me enough to work on. I can put a quote together for you and email it through by Friday. Is that ok?

B: Ja, das ist perfekt. Ich gebe Ihnen dann jetzt meine Email Adresse.

A: Thank you. I'll get back to you by Friday.

DIALOGUE 14 • B

B is going to launch a new catering business. A is a freelance website developer. B calls to find out how much a professional website would cost her and how quickly it could be done.

A: Web Solutions, A Jackson am Apparat.

B: Hi A. My name is B. I need a website and I've just found your details online. I'd like to have a chat to you about maybe building a site for me. Would you be interested in giving me a quote?

A: Aber sicher doch. Was genau haben Sie sich vorgestellt?

B: Well I'm about to launch a new catering business and I need to promote it. We specialise in vegan banquets so we want a really fresh look and feel, with lots of images of the food and ingredients.

A: OK. Haben Sie bereits Fotos oder müsste ich die Bilder zur Verfügung stellen?

B: We've just had a professional photoshoot done so I'll provide all the pictures. We've had some work done on branding too so I can give you some guidelines for the design.

A: OK super. Die Kosten hängen davon ab, wie komplex das Layout der Website werden soll. Haben Sie sich bereits Gedanken darüber gemacht, was alles beinhaltet werden soll?

B: Well there will need to be a map showing which areas we service. We'll also need a few pages to talk about what we do and the kind of ingredients we use, plus some sample menus. I also want a blog section, with links to all our social media feeds – Pinterest, Instagram, Facebook etc.

A: OK, das ist eigentlich alles ziemlich eindeutig. Wollen Sie, dass Kunden auf der Seite auch Buchungen durchführen können, oder wollen Sie Besucher lieber dazu ermutigen, Sie zuerst zu kontaktieren, wenn sie Anfragen haben?

B: Oh no, we'll handle the bookings directly with the clients, so we just want them to contact us, by phone or email.

A: Das hört sich gut an und gibt mir genügend, womit ich arbeiten kann. Ich kann bis Freitag ein Angebot für Sie zusammenstellen und es Ihnen dann per Email schicken. Wäre das in Ordnung?

B: Yes that's great. I'll give you my email address now.

A: Vielen Dank. Ich melde mich dann am Freitag.

DIALOGUE 15 • A

A is the office manager for a legal firm and B works for an electronics retailer. A needs to buy tablets for all the professionals in the firm and calls B to negotiate a special rate for a bulk purchase of the devices.

A: Smith Electronics, this is A. How can I help?

B: Hi A. Mein Name ist B. Ich arbeite bei General Accounting Firm und möchte gerne ein paar Tablets für die Angestellten in unserem Team kaufen.

A: I can definitely help you with that. How many do you need?

B: 14. Wir brauchen auch Schutzhüllen und drahtlose Tastaturen. Verkaufen Sie die auch?

A: Yes we stock the covers and keyboards too. I'm not sure if we could do 14 in the same colour though. Does that matter?

B: Nein, überhaupt nicht. Alle Farben sind in Ordnung.

A: OK great. So do you have a particular brand of tablet in mind? What sort of price range are you looking for?

B: Wir wollen etwas im mittleren Preisbereich, das gut mit Microsoft Office Applications läuft, damit unsere Angestellten es auch benützen können, wenn sie beim Kunden im Büro arbeiten. Was die Marke betrifft, können Sie mir gerne etwas empfehlen

A: Well we've got several that will meet your needs, and two of those are on sale at the moment, so you'll get a good deal. If you give me your email address I'll send you through the product specs right now.

B: Super, danke. Können Sie uns vielleicht auch einen Sonderpreis anbieten, da wir ja einen Großeinkauf bei Ihnen machen würden?

A: Yes of course. I'm not sure how much I can discount the tablets as they're already on sale, but I'll see what I can do. And I can certainly offer you a special price on all the accessories. How are you planning to pay?

B: Wir haben ein Geschäftskonto bei Ihnen. Können Sie mir bitte ein schriftliches Angebot schicken, damit ich einen Einkaufsauftrag einreichen kann?

A: Yes, sure. I'll email these product specifications to you now. Once you decide which type you want just call back and let me know, and I'll put the quote together right away.

B: Perfekt, vielen Dank A.

DIALOGUE 15 • B

A is the office manager for a legal firm and B works for an electronics retailer. A needs to buy tablets for all the professionals in the firm and calls B to negotiate a special rate for a bulk purchase of the devices.

A: Smith Electronics, A am Apparat. Wie kann ich Ihnen helfen?

B: Hi A. My name is B. I'm calling from the General Accounting Firm and I'm looking to buy some tablets for our professional team.

A: Da kann ich Ihnen auf jeden Fall helfen. Wieviele würden Sie brauchen?

B: 14. We also need protective covers and wireless keyboards. Do you sell those?

A: Ja, wir haben Hüllen auf Lager, und Tastaturen auch. Ich bin mir aber nicht sicher, ob wir 14 in der selben Farbe haben. Ist das wichtig?

B: Not at all. Any colours are fine.

A: OK super. Haben Sie sich irgendein besonderes Tablet vorgestellt? In was für einem Preisbereich würden Sie gerne bleiben?

B: We want something mid-range that will run Microsoft Office applications well, so our professionals can use them when they're out working at clients' offices. I'm happy to take your recommendation on the brand.

A: Na gut, wir haben ein paar Modelle, die allen Ihren Bedürfnissen entsprechen. Zwei davon sind gerade im Sonderverkauf, da könnten Sie also einen guten Deal bekommen. Wenn Sie mir Ihre Email Adresse geben wollen, dann kann ich Ihnen schnell ein paar Details über die Produkte schicken.

B: Great, thank you. And can you offer us a discount price, since we're planning to buy in bulk?

A: Ja natürlich. Ich bin mir nicht ganz sicher, wieviel ich Ihnen auf die Tablets nachlassen kann, nach dem sie bereits einen Sonderpreis haben, aber ich werde auf jeden Fall schaun, was ich machen kann. Und ich kann Ihnen auf alle Fälle einen Sonderpreis für das ganze Zubehör geben. Wie wollen Sie zahlen?

B: We have a corporate account with you. Can you provide a written quote please, so I can raise a purchase order?

A: Aber natürlich. Ich schicke Ihnen jetzt schnell die Produktdetails. Sobald Sie sich entschieden haben, welches Tablet sie wollen, rufen Sie mich einfach wieder an, und ich stelle dann sofort das Angebot zusammen.

B: Excellent. Thank you A.

DIALOGUE 16 • A

A is a freelance writer who is working on a project for B. She calls B to let him know that the first piece of work is ready for review and to talk about guidelines and deadlines for the next stage of the project.

A: Hi B. This is A. How are you?

B: Hi A. Mir geht es sehr gut, vielen Dank der Nachfrage. Wie geht es mit dem Projekt voran?

A: Really well. I'm actually calling to let you know that the first draft of the report is finished and ready for you to review. I've uploaded the file to our shared folder on the cloud server. I'd really appreciate your feedback when you have time to take a look.

B: Oh, das ist ja super. Gute Arbeit, dass Sie das vor Fristende fertig bekommen haben. Ich bin heute nachmittag total ausgebucht damit, ein Angebot zu bearbeiten, aber ich werde das Dokument gleich morgen früh durchlesen und werde Ihnen dann meine Kommentare schicken.

A: Thanks, I really appreciate it. I'll block out tomorrow afternoon to put through any amendments you'd like me to make.

B: Sehr gut, danke.

A: In the meantime, are you happy for me to start work on drafting the sales leaflets and the copy for the marketing emails?

B: Ja, fangen Sie doch bitte schonmal damit an. Haben Sie alle Informationen, die Sie dazu brauchen?

A: Actually no. I've got all the background information but I'll need the specifics of the deal you want to promote in the leaflets and emails. Can you provide me with the product launch dates and special pricing packages?

B: Aber natürlich. Ich werde dem Marketing Team gleich sagen, dass sie Ihnen die Daten rüberschicken sollen.

A: Thank you.

B: Ach übrigens, ich brauche zwei Versionen von jeder Email – eine für bestehende Kunden und eine für mögliche neue Kunden, die ihr Interesse auf der Website kundgetan haben. Die zwei Emails werden ziemlich ähnlich sein, nur der erste Paragraph muss abgeändert werden.

A: I'll get started now, and wait for your feedback on the report tomorrow.

DIALOGUE 16 • B

A is a freelance writer who is working on a project for B. She calls B to let him know that the first piece of work is ready for review and to talk about guidelines and deadlines for the next stage of the project.

A: Hi B. Ich bin es, A. Wie geht es Ihnen?

B: Hi A. I'm very well thanks. How is the work going on the project?

A: Wirklich gut. Ich rufe eigentlich sogar an, um Ihnen Bescheid zu geben, dass der erste Entwurf des Berichts fertig für Sie zur Durchsicht ist. Ich habe die Datei in unseren freigegebenen Ordner auf dem Cloud Server geladen. Bitte geben Sie mir Ihr Feedback wenn Sie Zeit gehabt haben, es durchzulesen.

B: Oh that's great. Well done for getting that completed ahead of schedule. I'm flat out working on a proposal this afternoon, but I'll review the document first thing tomorrow and get back to you with my comments.

A: Danke, das ist sehr nett. Ich werde mir morgen nachmittag freihalten damit ich sofort jegliche Änderungen machen kann, die Sie möglicherweise gerne hätten.

B: Excellent. Thanks.

A: Soll ich in der Zwischenzeit an den Entwürfen für die Verkaufsbroschüren und die Kopie für die Marketing Emails arbeiten?

B: Yes, please make a start on those. Do you have all the information you need?

A: Eigentlich nicht. Ich habe die ganzen Hintergrundinfos, aber ich brauche noch die spezifischen Details des Deals, den Sie mit dieser Broschüre und der Email anwerben wollen. Können Sie mir den Einführungstermin des Produkts geben und spezielle Preispakete?

B: Oh yes, I'll get the marketing team to email that data over to you right away.

A: Vielen Dank.

B: By the way, we'll need two versions of each email – one for existing customers and one for new prospects who express interest through the website. They will be very similar, just the opening paragraph will need to be different.

A: Ich fange sofort an, und warte dann auf Ihr Feedback für den Bericht morgen.

DIALOGUE 17 • A

A has changed his mind about a purchase and wishes to return the item to the shop. B is the sales representative who explains that the store's policy is to offer credit or exchange but not refunds for change of mind purchases. A accepts an exchange.

A: Hi. I'm wondering if you can help me, please?

B: Aber gerne. Was kann ich für Sie tun?

A: I bought this shredding machine yesterday, but when I got it back to the office I realised it's not suitable.

B: Ist das Gerät kaputt?

A: No, but it's just not robust enough for our needs. Apparently we need a secure cross-cut shredder, with the capacity to shred at least 20 pages at a time.

B: Wurde dieser Aktenvernichter jemals benutzt?

A: No, it's still in the original packaging and as you can see it hasn't even been opened. And I have the receipt right here.

B: Ok, vielen Dank. Leider ist die Regelung in unserem Laden, dass wir keine Rückerstattungen durchführen wenn Sie Ihre Meinung ändern. Ich kann Ihnen aber einen Umtausch anbieten, oder eine Ladengutschrift. Wäre das in Ordnung?

A: Yes, absolutely. Could you please show me some of your other shredders; hopefully you have something more suitable for us.

B: Aber gerne doch. Wir haben drei verschiedene querschnitts Aktenvernichter. Diese zwei hier sind ziemlich klein, aber der hier kann bis zu 25 Seiten auf einmal vernichten, und ist außerdem sehr schnell. Es gibt auch noch ein noch teureres Modell, das hat ein automatisches Papierzuführsystem, aber das müssten wir bestellen, da wir es leider nicht auf Lager haben.

A: No thanks, this one looks ideal. How much is it?

B: Der kostet $125, Sie müssten also noch $54 zahlen, wenn Sie Ihren alten eintauschen.

A: That's fine. I'll take it.

B: Okay. Dann führe ich jetzt erstmal die Rückgabe durch. Füllen Sie bitte Ihren Namen und die Adresse hier in dieses Formular, ich hole meinen Manager, damit er sein OK gibt. Dann kann ich den Verkauf des neuen Gerätes durchführen.

A: OK, thank you.

DIALOGUE 17 • B

A has changed his mind about a purchase and wishes to return the item to the shop. B is the sales representative who explains that the store's policy is to offer credit or exchange but not refunds for change of mind purchases. A accepts an exchange.

A: Hi. Können Sie mir vielleicht helfen?

B: Yes sir, what can I do for you?

A: Ich habe gestern diesen Aktenvernichter gekauft, aber als ich zurück ins Büro gekommen bin, habe ich festgestellt, dass er nicht passt.

B: Is the machine defective?

A: Nein, aber es ist einfach nicht robust genug für unsere Bedürfnisse. Offensichtlich brauchen wir einen sicheren querschnitts Aktenvernichter mit einer Kapazität von mindestens 20 Seiten pro Durchgang.

B: Has this shredder been used at all?

A: Nein, er ist auch noch in der Originalverpackung und wie Sie sehen können ist er auch nicht ausgepackt worden. Und ich habe die Quittung auch hier.

B: OK, thank you. Unfortunately our store policy is not to offer refunds for change-of-mind purchases. I can offer you an exchange though, or a store credit note. Would that be acceptable?

A: Ja, absolut. Können Sie mir bitte ein paar Ihrer anderen Aktenvernichter zeigen, hoffentlich gibt es da etwas passenderes für uns.

B: Certainly. We have three models of cross-cut shredder. These two are quite small, but this one takes up to 25 pages at a time and is very fast. There's a more expensive model available too, which comes with an automatic paper feeder, but we'd have to order that in for you as it's not in stock.

A: Nein danke, dieser hier sieht perfekt aus. Wieviel kostet er?

B: It's $125, so there would be an additional $54 to pay if you exchange yours for it.

A: Das passt. Ich nehme ihn.

B: OK, I'll just process the return for you first. Could you please fill in your name and address details on this form, and I'll get my manager to sign it off. Then I can process the sale of the new machine.

A: OK, vielen Dank.

DIALOGUE 18 • A

A is looking for a financial advisor and calls an accounting firm to learn more about their services. B is the business development manager who answers A queries and arranges to meet with him.

A: Hi, you're through to A Jackson. I'm the business development manager here at Accounting Associates. I understand you're looking for some information about our services?

B: Hallo A. Ja, bitte. Ihre Empfangsdame hat gesagt, dass Sie die richtige Person sind, mit der ich über die Konten für mein Unternehmen reden soll.

A: I certainly am. Before we get started, could I ask your name please?

B: Ja, mein Name ist B Green.

A: Thank you. And may I ask where you heard about us?

B: Ja, einer Ihrer Kunden ist ein Freund von mir. Er hat mir empfohlen, Sie anzurufen.

A: Oh that's good to hear. So you need help with your business accounts?

B: Ja. Ich habe gerade mein eigenes Beratungsunternehmen gestartet, und ich muss meine ganze Buchhaltung und Rechnungsstellung richtig einrichten. Ich benötige auch Hilfe mit der Steuererklärung und Finanzberichten, und ich könnte auch etwas Steuerberatung brauchen, damit ich sicherlich auch alles richtig strukturiert habe.

A: We can help you with all of that. We specialise in accounting for small businesses and we can provide a complete bookkeeping service if you want it. Or if you'd prefer to take care of that in-house, we can help you choose and set up your accounting software and train you on how to use it efficiently.

B: Das hört sich großartig an.

A: Would you like an appointment to come in and discuss it? I'd like to learn more about your business and talk you through our services and pricing structure. I can come to your offices, if that would be more convenient for you than coming here?

B: Unser Büro ist eigentlich noch nicht ganz fertig eingerichtet, deswegen würde ich mich lieber bei Ihnen treffen. Wie wäre es mit Donnerstag oder Freitag? So gegen 11Uhr vormittag wäre ideal für mich.

A: Let's make it Thursday. I'm putting it in my diary now. I look forward to meeting you.

DIALOGUE 18 • B

A is looking for a financial advisor and calls an accounting firm to learn more about their services. B is the business development manager who answers A queries and arranges to meet with him.

A: Hi, Sie sprechen mit A Jackson. Ich bin der Akquisitions Manager hier bei Accounting Associates. Wenn ich richtig informiert bin hätten Sie gerne mehr Informationen über unsere Dienstleistungen?

B: Hi A. Yes, please. Your receptionist said you would be the right person to talk to about the accounts for my business.

A: Da sind Sie definitv an der richtigen Stelle bei mir. Bevor wir anfangen, können Sie mir bitte Ihren Namen geben?

B: Yes, it's B Green.

A: Vielen Dank. Und kann ich auch fragen, wie Sie über uns erfahren haben?

B: Yes, one of your clients is a friend of mine. He recommended that I give you a call.

A: Oh, das freut mich zu hören. Sie brauchen also Hilfe mit Ihren Geschäftskonten?

B: Yes. I've just launched my own consulting firm and I need to get all my bookkeeping and invoicing set up properly. I'll need help with my tax returns and financial reports too, and I could also use some tax advice to make sure I've structured everything properly.

A: Wir könnenIhnen gerne mit alle dem helfen. Wir sind Spezialisten im Bereich Buchhaltung für Kleinunternehmen, und wir können Ihnen einen kompletten Buchhaltungsservice anbieten, falls Sie das wollen. Oder falls Sie das lieber selbst übernehmen möchten, dann können wir Ihnen auch gerne nur dabei helfen, die richtige Buchhaltungssoftware auszusuchen, einzurichten und Ihnen zeigen, wie Sie die Software am besten verwenden.

B: That sounds great.

A: Möchten Sie gerne einen Termin ausmachen, um alles zu besprechen? Ich würde gerne noch ein paar mehr Informationen über Ihr Geschäft erfahren und Ihnen unsere Services und Preisstruktur etwas besser erklären. Ich kann auch gerne in Ihr Büro kommen, falls das für Sie besser wäre?

B: Actually our office is still being set up, so I'd rather come to you, please. How about Thursday or Friday? Around 11am on either day would be ideal for me.

A: Dann machen wir doch Donnerstag. Ich gebe es gleich in meinen Terminkalender ein. Ich freue mich, Sie zu treffen!

DIALOGUE 19 • A

A is an assistant who has just realised he made a mistake in a document that has gone out to a client. B is his boss. A explains to B what has happened and how he proposes to rectify the error.

A: Hi B, have you got a moment. I need to talk to you about something.

B: Aber klar. Kommen Sie doch rein und nehmen Sie Platz. Was gibt es?

A: I've just been reading back over the project proposal we sent to the Myer client yesterday afternoon, and I've noticed an error. I'm so sorry, but it was totally my mistake. I should have proofread it more closely before sending it out.

B: Was war der Fehler? Ist er schlimm?

A: We used a template from another proposal as the basis for this document, and I'm afraid I left some of last year's data in place when I updated the financial section. Some of the totals don't add up correctly, and the sales projection figures are wrong.

B: Oh nein, das lässt uns aber nicht gerade professionell aussehen.

A: Yes, I know. I'm so sorry. I feel really bad about it.

B: Keine Sorge. Wenigstens ist der Fehler nur in der ergänzenden Information, nicht im Angebot selber oder dem Projektparameter. Und wir hatten es alle eilig, das Dokument fertig zu bekommen und rechtzeitig zu senden. Diese Dinge passieren leider, und ich schätze es sehr, dass Sie gleich zu mir gekommen sind und mir Bescheid gegeben haben. Wie schlage Sie vor könnten wir die Situation begradigen?

A: Well I've already spoken to the client's secretary to explain my error, and she said that the project team haven't yet met to review the proposal. I've prepared an updated document with all the correct figures and she said she would make sure they receive the new version before their meeting, if I send it through this morning. Would you be happy for me to do that?

B: Ja. Ich würde allerdings das überarbeitete Dokument vorher noch gerne einmal durchsehen.

A: Yes of course. I've got a copy here for you to review.

B: Vielen Dank, gute Arbeit, A. Der Fehler ist wirklich unglücklich gewesen, aber Sie haben ihn sehr gut gehandhabt. Ich rufe Sie dann, wenn ich das Dokument gelesen habe, und gebe Ihnen Bescheid, dass Sie es losschicken können.

A: OK. Thanks for being so understanding. I'll be more careful next time.

DIALOGUE 19 • B

A is an assistant who has just realised he made a mistake in a document that has gone out to a client. B is his boss. A explains to B what has happened and how he proposes to rectify the error.

A: Hi B, haben Sie gerade einen Moment Zeit? Ich muss mit Ihnen etwas bereden.

B: Sure. Come in and take a seat. So what's the problem?

A: Ich habe gerade nochmal das Projektangebot durchgelesen, das wir gestern an den Myer Kunden geschickt haben, und mir ist ein Fehler aufgefallen. Es tut mir so leid, das war absolut nicht meine Absicht. Ich hätte es besser überprüfen sollen, bevor ich es rausgeschickt habe.

B: What was the error? Is it serious?

A: Wir haben eine Dokumentvorlage von einem anderen Angebot als Grundlage für dieses Dokument verwendet, und leider habe ich einige der letztjährigen Daten im Finanzteil des Dokuments gelassen, die ich aktualisieren hätte sollen. Einige der Gesamtsummen sind nicht ganz korrekt und die Umsatzerwartungsnummern sind falsch.

B: Oh dear. That's going to make us look very unprofessional.

A: Ja, ich weiß. Es tut mir wirklich leid, ich fühle mich sehr schlecht deshalb.

B: Don't worry A. At least the mistake is only in the supporting information, not in the quote or the project parameters. And we were all rushing to get that document finished and submitted by the deadline. This sort of thing happens, and I appreciate you coming to tell me so promptly. So what do you propose to do about it?

A: Also gut, ich habe bereits mit der Sekretärin des Kunden gesprochen und habe ihr meinen Fehler erklärt, und sie sagte, dass das Projektteam sich noch nicht getroffen hat, um das Angebot durchzusehen. Ich habe eine aktualisierte Version des Dokuments vorbereitet, mit all den richtigen Nummern, und sie hat gesagt, sie wird sicherstellen, dass das Team die neue Version vor ihrem Meeting erhält, wenn ich es noch heute morgen durchschicke. Soll ich das machen?

B: Yes. I'd like to check over the revised document first though please.

A: Ja, aber natürlich. Hier ist eine Kopie für Ihre Durchsicht.

B: Thank you, that's good work A. It's unfortunate about the mistake, but you handled this well. I'll call you once I've read through this document, to confirm you can send it.

A: OK. Vielen Dank für Ihr Verständnis. Ich werde beim nächsten Mal besser aufpassen.

DIALOGUE 20 • A

A is a business training consultant and B is the training manager at a small firm. B has sent an email enquiry and A is responding to try to sell him some services.

A: My name's A and I'm calling from Smart Business Training. You emailed us this morning about some training you're interested in, and I'd like to talk through how we can help you. Is now a good time?

B: Ja, ich habe gerade Zeit, darüber zu sprechen.

A: Great, so I see you're interested in our time management and productivity courses. Is the training for yourself?

B: Nein. Ich bin eigentlich der Schulungsmanager bei einer Rechtsfirma. Wir haben 12 Angestellte und 2 Verwaltungsangestellte, die gerne die Schulung besuchen würden. Können Sie uns einen hausinternen Kurs anb ieten, oder müßten sie einen der öffentlichen Workshops besuchen?

A: Yes, we can come to you and give a private training session. Those are both half-day courses, so if you like we can combine them into a single full-day experience, to save on travel and set up costs.

B: Oh ja, das wäre sehr hilfreich und auch weniger Unterbrechung als wenn wir jeden an zwei Tagen in Schulungen beschäftigt hätten. Können Sie mir ein bisschen mehr über Ihre Kurse erzählen?

A: Sure. We specialise in training for small professional firms, so the material is all tailored to businesses like yours. We focus on how to tackle the big issues all professionals face these days – constant distractions, email overload, and mastering the digital tools that can dramatically improve efficiency. We'll talk to you in advance about what software and email systems you use, so we can make sure everything is relevant.

B: Das hört sich doch super an. Arbeiten Sie mit Rollenspielen und Szenarios in Ihren Schulungen?

A: Yes – and we prefer to use real-life examples from your own business for those, so that they'll resonate with your participants. Training is far more effective when it makes direct sense in the context of your work.

B: Das hört sich doch perfekt an. Könnten Sie mir bitte die Kursbeschreibungen schicken, zusammen mit den Preisen, und mögliche Daten für einen Workshop im April?

A: Yes, I'll send them through to you right away. Thanks for your time.

DIALOGUE 20 • B

A is a business training consultant and B is the training manager at a small firm. B has sent an email enquiry and A is responding to try to sell him some services.

A: Mein Name ist A von Smart Business Training. Sie haben uns heute morgen eine Email geschickt bezüglich einiger Schulungen, an denen Sie interessiert sind, und ich würde gerne mit Ihnen darüber sprechen, wie wir Ihnen helfen könnten. Ist gerade eine gute Zeit dafür?

B: Yes, I'm free to discuss it now.

A: Super. Ich sehe hier also, dass Sie an unseren Kursen für Zeitmanagement und Produktivität interessiert sind. Wären die Kurse für Sie selber?

B: No. I'm actually the training manager at a legal firm. We have 12 professionals and 2 administrative staff members who would like to attend the training. Can you offer us an in-house training course, or will they need to attend one of your public workshops?

A: Ja, wir können gerne zu Ihnen kommen und Ihnen eine private Schulungssession geben. Das sind beides halb-Tages Kurse, wenn Sie wollen könnten wir das in eine ganz-Tages Schulung verbinden, was Ihnen Reise- und Organisationskosten sparen würde.

B: Oh yes, that would be helpful, and less disruptive than having everyone tied up in training on two separate days. So can you tell me a bit more about the courses?

A: Aber sicher doch. Wir spezialisieren uns auf Schulungen für kleine Unternehmen wie Ihres, das bedeutet, dass das Material alles auf Unternehmen wie Ihres zugeschnitten ist. Wir konzentrieren uns darauf, wie man all die großen Probleme, die alle Geschäftsleute heutzutage antreffen, am besten handhaben kann – permanente Ablenkungen, zu viele Emails, und wie man am besten die digitalen Instrumenten verwenden kann, um die Effizienz drastisch zu verbessern. Wir würden vorher mit Ihnen bereden, welche Software und welches Email System Sie verwenden, damit wir sicherstellen, dass alles passend ist.

B: Oh that sounds great. Do you use role plays and scenarios in your training?

A: Ja – und wir verwenden gerne Beispiele aus dem wirklichen Leben aus Ihrem Unternehmen dafür, das wirkt besser für Ihre Teilnehmer. Schulungen sind um einiges effektiver, wenn sie direkten Sinn machen im Kontext Ihrer Arbeit.

B: Well that does sound ideal. Could you please email me the course outlines and costings, and some possible dates in April for the workshop?

A: Ja, ich schicke Ihnen die Information gleich durch. Vielen Dank für Ihre Zeit.

DIALOGUE 21 • A

A wants to apply for a job. B is the recruitment consultant who answers his enquiry and talks him through the application process.

A: Right Job Recruitment, you're through to A.

B: Hi A. Mein Name ist B Black. Ich habe gerade eine Anzeige auf BestJobs.com gesehen für eine Stelle als Büromanager bei einer Buchhaltungsfirma. Ich würde mich gerne darauf bewerben.

A: Hi B. Thanks for calling. I'm managing the shortlist for that position, so you've come through to the right person.

B: Großartig. Können Sie mir bitte etwas mehr über die Position erzählen?

A: Certainly. It's for a medium-sized firm in the city centre. They have about 80 employees based at the site, and the office is always busy with clients coming and going. They want someone very calm and professional, with solid experience in a similar environment. What's your background?

B: Das hört sich sehr passend für mich an. Ich arbeite derzeit als Büromanager bei einer sehr belebten Rechtsfirma. Wir haben ca. 40 Angestellte und ein großes Verwaltungsteam, inkl. 5 Empfangsleuten, die sich um die Besucher kümmern.

A: Interesting. So why do you want to leave that role?

B: Naja, ich bin dort schon seit vier Jahren und ich suche einfach nach einer neuen Herausforderung. Außerdem ist die Lage nicht ideal – wir sind ziemlich weit entfernt von der Stadt in einem Industriegebiet, und ich würde gerne in einer etwas lebhafteren Umgebung arbeiten.

A: It does sound like you could be a good candidate for this role. Can you please tell me about your education and experience?

B: Ich habe Qualifikationen im Bereich der Betriebswirtschaftslehre und ich arbeite seit fast 10 Jahren im Büromanagement. Ich habe als Verwaltungsangestellter bei einer Schulungsfirma angefangen und wurde dann zum Manager befördert. Nach drei Jahren habe ich diese Stelle verlassen um den Job anzunehmen, bei dem ich aktuell arbeite – ich war einfach bereit für eine größere Herausforderung und es war ein guter Schritt für meine Karriere.

A: OK great, so I'll need to see your CV and talk through some more details before I can put you forward, but based on this conversation it sounds like I'll be able to shortlist you. Have you got time to come in for a quick interview with me this afternoon?

B: Ja, natürlich. Ich kann so gegen 14Uhr bei Ihnen im Büro sein.

A: Excellent. See you then.

DIALOGUE 21 • B

A wants to apply for a job. B is the recruitment consultant who answers his enquiry and talks him through the application process.

A: Right Job Recruitment, Sie sprechen mit A.

B: Hi A. My name is B Black, and I'm responding to an advert I've just seen in on the BestJobs.com website for an office manager at an accounting firm. I'd really like to apply.

A: Hi B. Vielen Dank für Ihren Anruf. Ich bin verantwortlich für die engere Auswahlliste für diese Stelle, Sie sind also genau bei der richtigen Person gelandet.

B: Great. Can you tell me a bit more about the job please?

A: Aber gerne doch. Die Position ist bei einem mittelständischen Unternehmen im Stadtzentrum. Es gibt dort etwa 80 Angestellte, und im Büro ist immer ein ständiger Fluß von Kunden. Die Firma sucht nach einer ruhigen und professionellen Person mit solider Erfahrung in einem ähnlichen Berufsfeld. Was ist Ihr beruflicher Hintergrund?

B: It sounds like a great fit, actually. I'm currently the office manager at a busy legal firm. We have around 40 professionals and a large team of supporting staff, including 5 receptionists to handle all the visitors.

A: Interessant. Und warum genau wollen Sie diese Stelle verlassen?

B: Well I've been here for four years and I'm looking for a new challenge. Plus the location isn't ideal – we're quite far out of town in a business park, and I'm keen to work in a more vibrant environment. I've been keeping my eye open for an exciting job in the CBD, and this opportunity looks ideal.

A: Es hört sich tatsächlich so an, als ob Sie ein guter Kandidat für diese Stelle sein könnten. Können Sie mir ein wenig über Ihre Ausbildung und Erfahrung erzählen?

B: I have qualifications in business administration, and I've been in office management for almost a decade. I started out as an office junior at a training company, then got promoted to manager. I left that role after three years to take on my current job – I was ready for a bigger challenge and it was a great career move.

A: OK, super. Ich müßte dann Ihren Lebenslauf sehen und noch ein paar andere Details mit Ihnen durchsprechen bevor ich Sie weiterleiten kann. Aber nachdem was Sie mir gerade erzählt haben sieht es so aus, als ob Sie es in die engere Auswahl schaffen können. Haben Sie heute nachmittag kurz Zeit für ein Vorstellungsgespräch mit mir?

B: Yes, sure. I can get to your offices by about 2pm.

A: Perfekt. Bis dann.

DIALOGUE 22 • A

A needs to rent some office space for a new business. B is the agent for a serviced office building, showing him the available space and demonstrating all the facilities.

A: Nice to meet you B. I'm A, the agent for the FreeSpace complex. Would you like to take a look around or do you have some questions first?

B: Hi A. Schön, Sie zu treffen. Schauen wir uns doch erst einmal um, ich stelle meine Fragen dann unterwegs.

A: OK great. So we'll start here with the shared reception area. As you can see, it's very smart and it's staffed by a very professional reception team. I guess you met them when you first arrived?

B: Ja; und sie waren sehr hilfreich und freundlich. Wieviele Mieter haben Sie hier in diesem Gebäude?

A: We have 16 office suites, and 12 are currently occupied, with another two companies moving in over the next month. Our tenants include lawyers, accountants and financial advisors, so it's a very busy and professional office. It's a great working environment.

B: Ja, so hört es sich an.

A: This is the shared facilities area. As you can see, we have the very latest in digital office technology - multimedia projectors, teleconferencing facilities and state-of-the-art document centres with secure printing facilities. There are five meeting rooms plus a large boardroom, which are all free for tenants to use. You just have to book them through reception.

B: Sehr beeindruckend. Kann ich bitte einen der Büroräume sehen?

A: Yes, number seven here is available, or we have a larger unit available upstairs if you need more space. Each suite is fully equipped with ergonomic office furniture and cutting edge telecoms and wifi services.

B: Das sieht perfekt aus. Was sind die Mietkosten und Servicegebühren, die ich erwarten kann?

A: That will depend on the suite size and the length of the tenancy agreement. Let's just pop into my office and I'll show you the rental documents.

B: OK, vielen Dank B.

DIALOGUE 22 • B

A needs to rent some office space for a new business. B is the agent for a serviced office building, showing him the available space and demonstrating all the facilities.

A: Es freut mich, Sie zu treffen,B. Mein Name ist A, ich bin der Makler hier für das FreeSpace Gebäude. Möchten Sie sich lieber zuerst umsehen oder haben Sie gleich Fragen?

B: Hi A. Great to meet you. Let's take a look and I'll ask my questions as we go.

A: Okay, gerne. Fangen wir doch hier an mit dem geteilten Empfangsbereich. Wie Sie sehen können ist er sehr gepflegt und das Empfangsteam ist auch sehr professionell. Ich nehme an, Sie haben sie getroffen, als Sie angekommen sind?

B: Yes, they were very helpful and friendly. How many tenants do you have in this complex?

A: Wir haben 16 Büroräume. 12 sind derzeit vermietet, und zwei weitere Firmen ziehen im nächsten Monat ein. Unsere Mieter sind Rechtsanwälte, Buchhalter und Finanzberater, es ist also immer geschäftig und sehr professionell hier. Eine sehr gute Arbeitsumgebung.

B: Yes, it sounds like it.

A: Hier finden Sie die geteilten Einrichtungen. Wie Sie sehen können haben wir die allerneusten Geräte was digitale Bürotechnik betrifft – Multimediaprojektoren, Telekonferenzeinrichtungen und die allermodernsten Dokumentzentren mit sicheren Druckereinrichtungen. Es gibt fünf Konferenzräume und einen großen Sitzungssaal, die alle für unsere Mieter umsonst sind. Sie müssen sie einfach nur durch unser Empfangsteam buchen.

B: Impressive. Can I see one of the office suites please?

A: Ja, Nummer 7 hier ist verfügbar, oder wir haben auch eine größere Einheit im oberen Stockwerk verfügbar, falls Sie mehr Raum benötigen. Jedes der Büros ist komplett ausgestattet mit ergonomischen Büromöbeln und modernen Telekom und WLAN Services.

B: This looks ideal. So what rental costs and service charges can I expect?

A: Das kommt auf die Größe des Büros an und die Länge des Mietvertrags. Gehen wir einfach in mein Büro und dann kann ich Ihnen die Mietunterlagen zeigen.

B: OK, thanks A.

DIALOGUE 23 • A

A wants to get some business strategy advice but doesn't know who to ask. B is his accountant. B gives A some advice on what to look for and recommends a firm she has used before.

A: Hi B. This is A White. I'm just wondering if I could ask you for some quick advice.

B: Hi A, schön von Ihnen zu hören. Wie kann ich helfen?

A: I'm getting ready to launch that business we discussed at our last review meeting, and I really need some guidance. I'm finding it really hard to put together my business plan and financial projections, and I'm just not sure that my marketing and commercialisation strategies are quite on track. I need to talk to a business consultant, but I have no idea who to turn to.

B: Das freut mich zu hören, dass Ihre Pläne langsam Form annehmen. Ich bin davon überzeugt, dass Sie hier ein echt gutes Konzept am Start haben. Es ist eine gute Idee, sich in dieser Phase etwas Beratung zu holen – es ist immer gut, von Anfang an auf dem richtigen Weg zu sein. Für mich hört es sich so an, als ob Sie eher etwas mit einem Unternehmensmentor anfangen könnten als einer Beratungsfirma – jemand der auf lange Zeit gesehen mit Ihnen zusammen arbeitet, und der Ihr Unternehmen richtig gut kennenlernt.

A: Yes, I like the sound of that. I'd definitely rather deal with just one person.

B: Ich finde eigentlich immer, dass für jemanden wie Sie, der zwar eine großartige Idee hat, aber nicht wirklich viel Erfahrung darin, ein Geschäft zu starten oder zu managen, dies der beste Weg ist. Ein Mentor bleibt an Ihrer Seite für die gesamte Zeit, er hilft Ihnen mit allen Herausforderungen die sich Ihnen entgegenstellen werden innerhalb der nächsten paar Jahre. Ich denke, dass ist speziell in Ihrem Fall besonders wichtig, weil Sie versuchen, in einem besonders schnelllebigen, high-tech Markt Fuß zu fassen. Sie brauchen auf alle Fälle jemanden an Ihrer Seite, der Ihnen dabei helfen kann, auf die Veränderungen zu reagieren und Ihr Geschäftsmodell und –strategie auf die sich ändernden Bedürfnisse Ihrer Kunden anzupassen.

A: Yes! That's exactly what I want. So can you recommend anyone?

B: Zufälligerweise weiß ich genau die richtige Person für diesen Job. Er hat bereits mit einigen meiner Kunden in den letzten paar Jahren zusammengearbeitet, und die haben ihn alle in den höchsten Tönen gelobt. Die Leute und die Unternehmen, mit denen er arbeitet, scheinen ihm wirklich am Herzen zu liegen, und er hat selber seit über 30 Jahren erfolgreiche Unternehmen geführt. Ich bin davon überzeugt, dass er Ihnen helfen kann.

A: Great, can you email me his details please, and I'll give him a call right away. Thanks so much for your help Beatrice!

B: Gern geschehen. Es war nett, mit Ihnen zu plaudern. Viel Glück!

A: Thank you.

DIALOGUE 23 • B

A wants to get some business strategy advice but doesn't know who to ask. B is his accountant. B gives A some advice on what to look for and recommends a firm she has used before.

A:	Hi B. A. White am Apparat. Ich habe mich gefragt, ob ich Sie ganz schnell um Rat fragen kann.

B:	Hi A, great to hear from you. How can I help?

A:	Ich bin kurz davor, mein Geschäft zu starten, über das wir in unserem letzten Meeting gesprochen haben, und ich brauche etwas Beratung. Ich habe wirklich Probleme damit, meinen Geschäftsplan und die Finanzprognosen zusammenzustellen. Und ich bin mir auch nicht ganz sicher, ob meine Marketing und Vermarktungsstrategien die richtigen sind. Ich muss einfach mal mit einem Unternehmensberater sprechen, aber ich habe keine Ahnung, an wen ich mich da wenden soll.

B:	Oh I'm glad that your plans are starting to come together. I think you've got a great concept there. It's a good idea to get some advice at this stage - far better to get on the right track from the start. It sounds to me like you'd be better off with a business mentor rather than a consulting firm – someone who will work with you for the long term, and really get to know your business well.

A:	Ja, das hört sich gut an. Ich würde definitv lieber nur mit einer Person dealen.

B:	I always think that's the best way to go for someone like you, who has a great idea but not much experience in launching or running a business. A mentor will stick with you throughout the journey, and help you with all the challenges you'll face over the next few years. I think that's even more important in your case, since you're hoping to break into such a fast moving, high-tech market. You'll need someone by your side who can help you react to changes and evolve your business model and strategy as the needs of your customers change.

A:	Ja! Das ist genau das, was ich will! Also, können Sie jemanden empfehlen?

B:	Actually I do know someone I think would be ideal. He's worked with a couple of my clients over the past few years and they've spoken extremely highly of him. He really seems to care about the people and businesses he works with, and he's been running successful businesses himself for over 30 years. I think he'll really be able to help you.

A:	Super, können Sie mir bitte seine Kontaktdaten emailen, dann rufe ich ihn gleich an. Vielen Dank nochmal, Beatrice!

B:	My pleasure. Lovely to talk to you. Good luck!

A:	Danke.

DIALOGUE 24 • A

A is a marketing consultant who has worked with B in the past. They haven't had any contact in a while so A calls to find out if there is anything B needs, and to inform her of her new services

A: Hi B, this is A from Expert Marketing. It's been a while since we spoke, so I just thought I'd call and see how everything's going for you.

B: Hi A. Schön von Ihnen zu hören. Wie geht es Ihnen?

A: I'm well thanks B. So what's been happening? Is business going well?

B: Jetzt, wo Sie fragen, eigentlich ja. Ich bin in letzter Zeit wirklich sehr beschäftigt gewesen. Die Werbecampagne hat sich echt bezahlt gemacht, und die hergestellt haben, waren ein großer Erfolg.

A: Oh I'm really glad to hear that. Have you made any progress with your website yet?

B: Ja, wir sind jetzt endlich online mit der Seite, aber leider haben wir nicht wirklich viel damit gemacht. Sie ist definitv auf meiner Liste, aber ich weiß ehrlichgesagt nicht so genau, wo ich anfangen soll.

A: Oh. Well I was actually calling to let you know about a new service we've just launched, which sounds like it might be of interest to you in the circumstances. We've just hired an marketing specialist, and we're offering a new suite of digital services for small businesses like yours. We can help you with optimising your website, content marketing and managing your social media accounts.

B: Das hört sich interessant an. Und wie genau generiert das Geschäft?

A: It's a powerful new strategy for generating business leads. It involves creating content for your website that will attract visitors who need the kind of services you offer. It can be blog posts, free downloads, white papers, videos and so on. Images and multimedia content are very popular at the moment. Sharing useful information on relevant topics shows people that you have something of value to offer them.

B: Großartig. Das hört sich genau danach an, was ich brauche. Können Sie vielleicht in mein Büro kommen, damit wir etwas genauer darüber sprechen können? Vielleicht am Freitag so gegen 14Uhr nachmittag?

A: Absolutely. I'll see you then. Thanks.

DIALOGUE 24 • B

A is a marketing consultant who has worked with B in the past. They haven't had any contact in a while so A calls to find out if there is anything B needs, and to inform her of her new services

A: Hi B, hier spricht A von Expert Marketing. Wir haben schon seit einiger Zeit nichts mehr voneinander gehört. Deshalb wollte ich mal kurz anrufen und hören, wie es so bei Ihnen läuft?

B: Hi A. Good to hear from you. How are you?

A: Mir geht es gut, vielen Dank, B. Und, was ist so los bei Ihnen? Läuft das Geschäft gut?

B: Actually yes, we've been really busy lately. The advertising campaign has really paid off, and the promotional materials you created for us have been a huge success.

A: Oh, das freut mich sehr zu hören. Haben Sie schon irgendwelche Fortschritte mit Ihrer Website gemacht?

B: Yes, we've got the site online at last, but I'm afraid we haven't done much with it yet. It's on my to-do list, but I'm not really sure where to start, to be honest.

A: Oh. Ich habe Sie eigentlich angerufen, um Ihnen über unseren neuen Service zu erzählen, den wir gerade gestartet haben. Der könnte unter Umständen interessant für Sie sein. Wir haben gerade einen Marketing Spezialisten eingestellt und bieten jetzt eine Reihe von digitalen Dienstleistungen für Kleinunternehmen wie Ihres an. Wir können Ihnen dabei helfen, Ihre Website und Ihr Content-Vermarktung zu optimieren und Ihre Social Media Konten zu verwalten.

B: Sounds interesting. So how does that generate business?

A: Also gut, der Inhalt lockt die Leute zu Ihrer Website und dort werden dann ihre Kontaktinfos eingesammelt. Dafür bekommen sie z.B. einen gratis Download. Sehr effektiv, weil es die Leute anlockt, die wirklich an dem, was Sie anzubieten haben, interessiert sind. Das führt dann wiederum zu qualitativ hochwertigeren Leads und um einiges bessere Umrechnungsraten.

B: Great. It sounds like just what we need. Could you come in for a meeting to talk me through it? Are you free at around 2pm on Friday afternoon?

A: Absolut. Wir sehen uns dann am Freitag. Vielen Dank!

DIALOGUE 25 • A

A is the accounts clerk for a company and B is the client. A calls B to chase up payment on an unpaid invoice.

A: Accounts Department, A speaking.

B: Hi A. Hier ist B von Expert Marketing. Ich wollte Sie nur kontaktieren um etwas über eine Rechnung vom letzten Monat herauszufinden. Sind Sie da der beste Ansprechpartner dafür?

A: Yes, I can help you with that. Do you have the invoice number to hand?

B: Ja, die Rechnungsnummer ist INV-37601. Sie wurde am 18. Dezember rausgeschickt.

A: Just a moment, I'm just logging in to our payment system to check whether we have received it. What amount was it for?

B: $18 570. Die Rechnung war für eine Jahresendsmarketingstrategie und die Anzeigenfläche, die Sie in den Weihnachtsausgaben aller Fachzeitschriften gekauft haben. Die Zahlung war am 31. Dezember fällig, wir brauchen die Zahlung also eher dringend, damit wir die Konten mit diesen Zeitschriften ausgleichen können.

A: Ah yes, here it is. I see it was received on December 19th and sent to the Communications Department for authorisation. Let me just check if we ever received back the signed copy.

B: Vielen Dank.

A: Oh it's right here in the pile for processing today. I'm so sorry for the delay - it looks like the Marketing Director has only just returned from vacation, as there's a whole stack of authorised invoices here. It must have been waiting on her desk all this time.

B: Ah, okay. Sie wird also heute gezahlt?

A: Yes, I'll process it for priority payment immediately. The funds should be in your account by tomorrow morning.

B: Super, das ist großartig. Vielen Dank für Ihre Hilfe A.

A: It's my pleasure B. I'm so sorry the invoice wasn't paid on time.

DIALOGUE 25 • B

A is the accounts clerk for a company and B is the client. A calls B to chase up payment on an unpaid invoice.

A: Buchhaltungsabteilung, A am Apparat.

B: Hi A. This is B from Expert Marketing. I'm just contacting you to enquire about an invoice from last month. Are you the best person to speak to about it?

A: Ja, da kann ich Ihnen weiterhelfen. Haben Sie vielleicht gerade die Rechnungsnummer parat?

B: Yes, it is INV-37601. It was sent on 17 December.

A: Einen kleinen Moment. Ich muss mich ganz schnell in unserem Zahlungssytem anmelden um zu sehen, ob wir die Rechnung erhalten haben. Was war der Betrag?

B: $18 570. It was for the year-end marketing strategy and the advertising you purchased in the Christmas editions of all the trade magazines. It was due for payment by December 31, and we urgently need to take payment so we can settle accounts with those publications.

A: Ah ja, hier ist sie. Ich sehe hier, dass wir sie am 20. Dezember erhalten haben und sie dann weiter an die Communications Abteilung zur Authorisierung geschickt haben. Lassen Sie mich schnell sehen, ob wir jemals eine unterschriebene Kopie zurückbekommen haben.

B: Thank you.

A: Ah, hier ist sie, direkt im Stapel für die heutige Bearbeitung. Es tut mir so leid, dass es so lange gedauert hat – es sieht so aus, als ob der Marketingleiter erst vor kurzem aus dem Urlaub zurückgekommen ist, weil ich hier einen ganzen Stapel authorisierter Rechnungen haben. Ihre Rechnung hat wahrscheinlich die ganze Zeit auf ihrem Schreibtisch gelegen.

B: Oh I see. So will it be paid today?

A: Ja, ich werde sie sofort zur Zahlung bearbeiten. Das Geld sollte morgen auf Ihrem Konto sein.

B: Ok that's great, thank you A. I appreciate your help.

A: Es war mein Vergnügen, B. Und entschuldigung nochmal für die Verspätung.